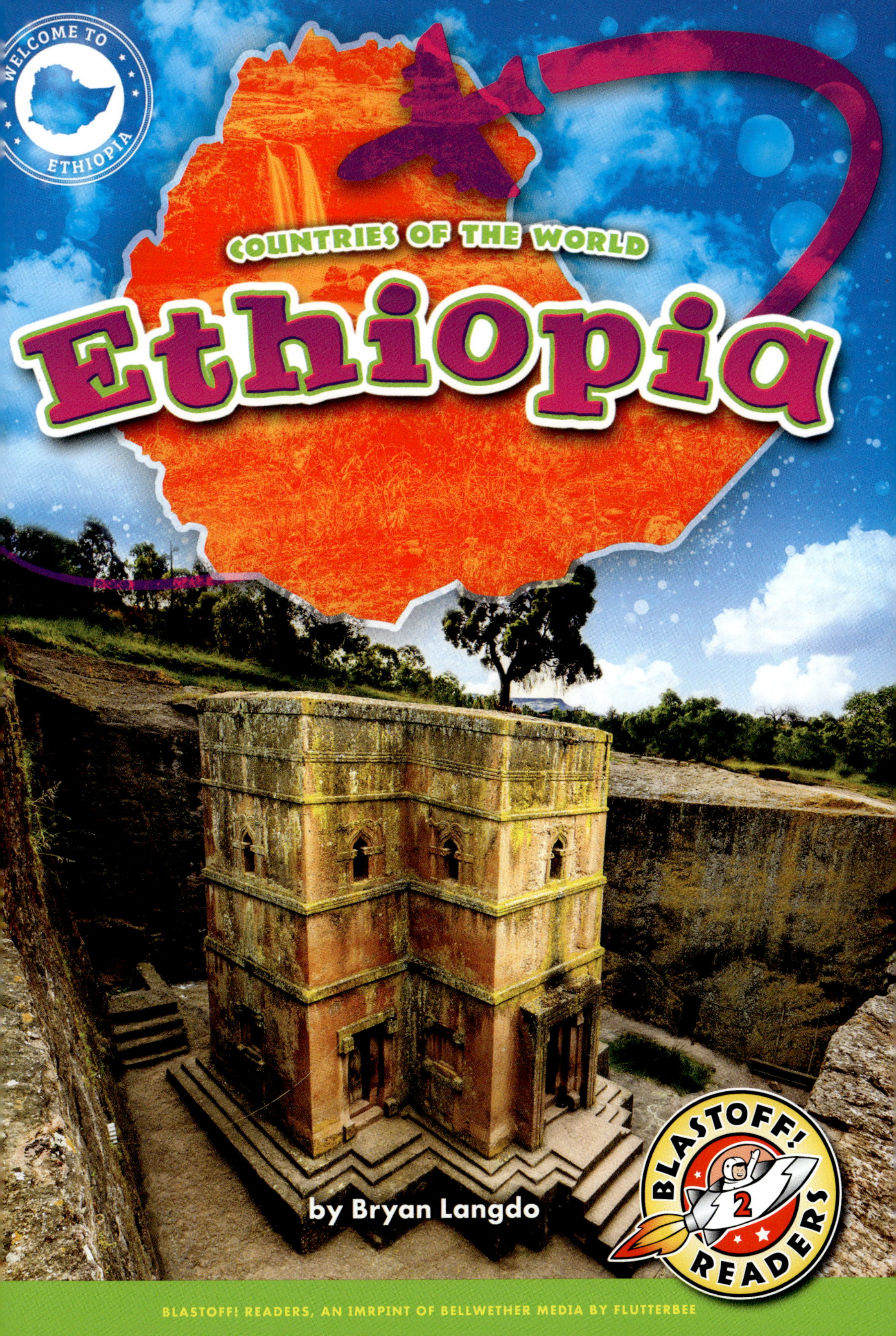
WELCOME TO
ETHIOPIA
COUNTRIES OF THE WORLD
Ethiopia
by Bryan Langdo
BLASTOFF!
2
READERS
BLASTOFF! READERS, AN IMRPINT OF BELLWETHER MEDIA BY FLUTTERBEE

Blastoff! Readers are carefully developed by literacy experts to build reading stamina and move students toward fluency by combining standards-based content with developmentally appropriate text.

Level 1 provides the most support through repetition of high-frequency words, light text, predictable sentence patterns, and strong visual support.

Level 2 offers early readers a bit more challenge through varied sentences, increased text load, and text-supportive special features.

Level 3 advances early-fluent readers toward fluency through increased text load, less reliance on photos, advancing concepts, longer sentences, and more complex special features.

★ **Blastoff! Universe**

Reading Level

Grade K

Grades 1–3

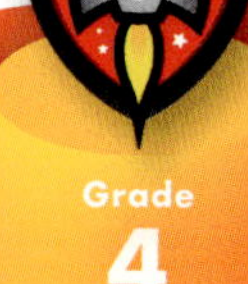

Grade 4

This edition first published in 2026 by Bellwether Media, Inc.

For information regarding permission, write to Bellwether Media, Inc., Attention: Permissions Department, 3500 American Blvd W, Suite 150, Bloomington, MN 55431.

Library of Congress Cataloging-in-Publication Data is available at www.loc.gov or upon request from the publisher.

ISBN: 9798893047820 (hardcover)
ISBN: 9798893048827 (paperback)

Editor: Rachael Barnes   Designer: Brittany McIntosh

Printed in the United States of America, North Mankato, MN.

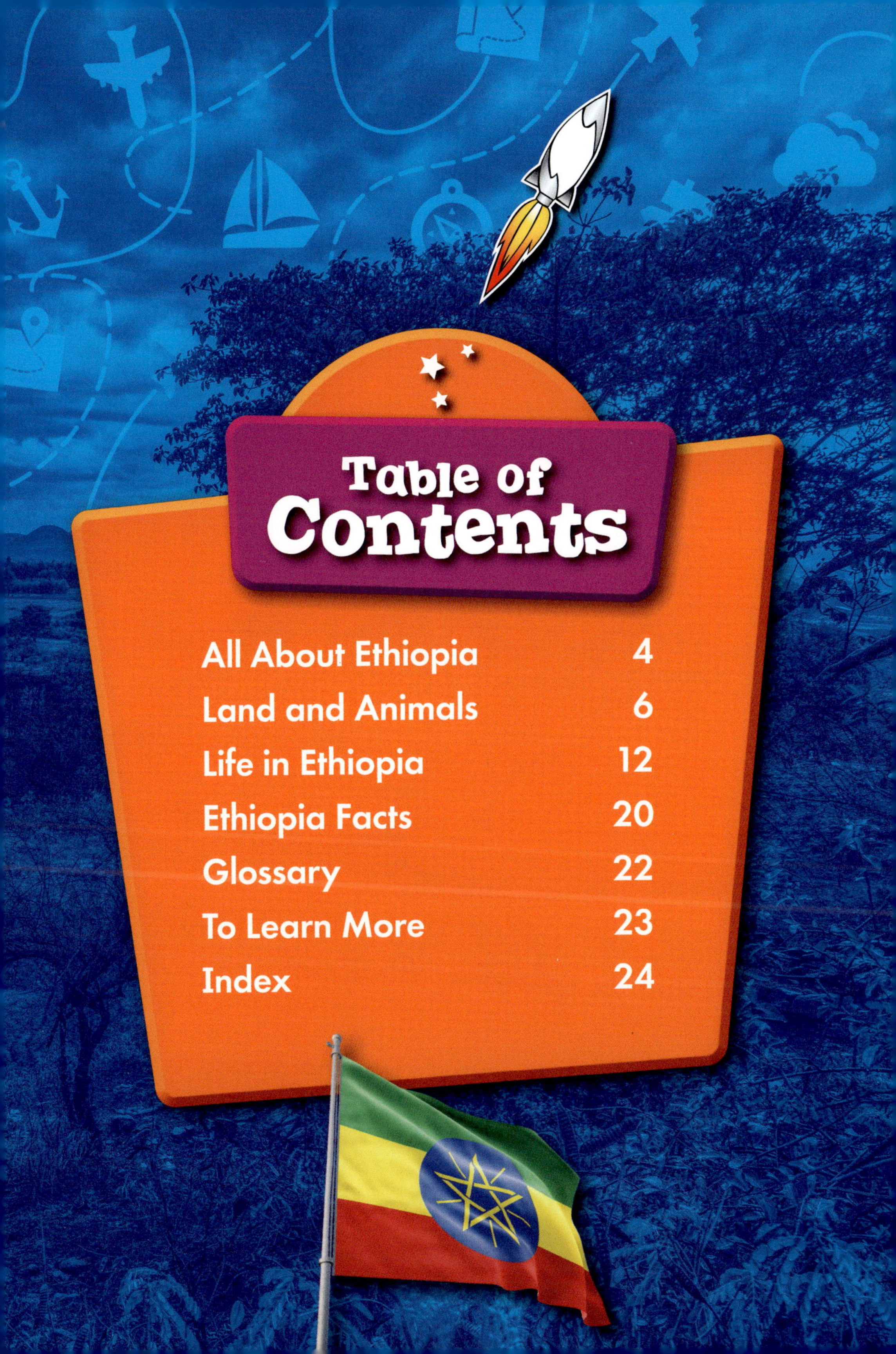

Table of Contents

All About Ethiopia

Ethiopia is a country in Africa.
It is part of the **Horn of Africa**.
Ethiopia's capital is Addis Ababa.

The country is known as the birthplace of coffee!

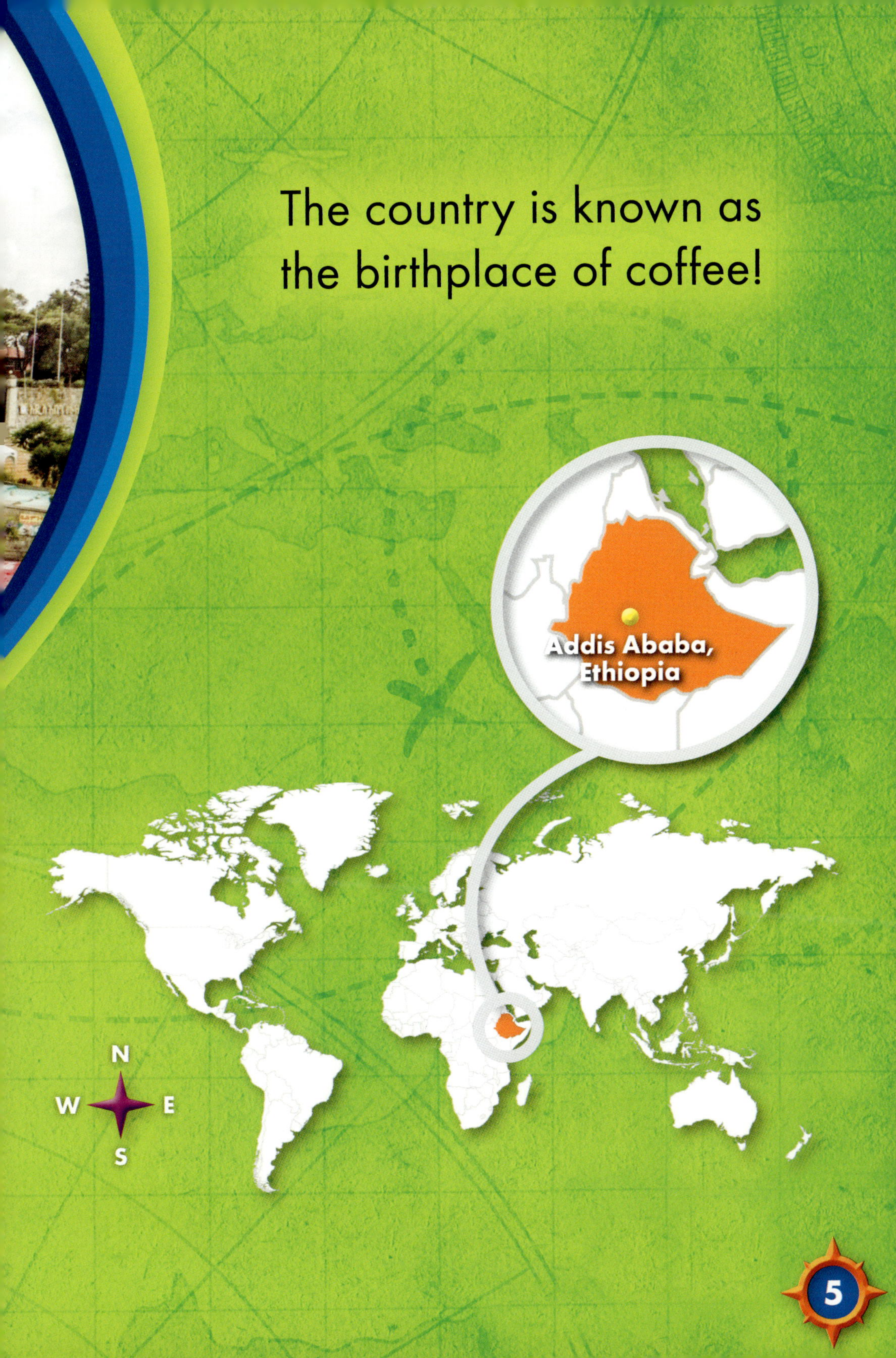

Land and Animals

Mountains and **plateaus** cover much of the country. Rivers flow down to the **plains**.

The Great Rift Valley separates the Eastern and Western Highlands.

Ras Dejen

Size: 14,905 feet (4,543 meters) tall
Famous For: highest point in Ethiopia and the Horn of Africa

Ethiopia's plains are hot and dry.
It is cooler in the mountains.

The country has two rainy seasons. Many plants grow during these months.

Monkeys eat leaves in Ethiopia's mountains. Ibex munch on grass nearby.

Wolves hunt alone in **grasslands**. Turacos fly in forests.

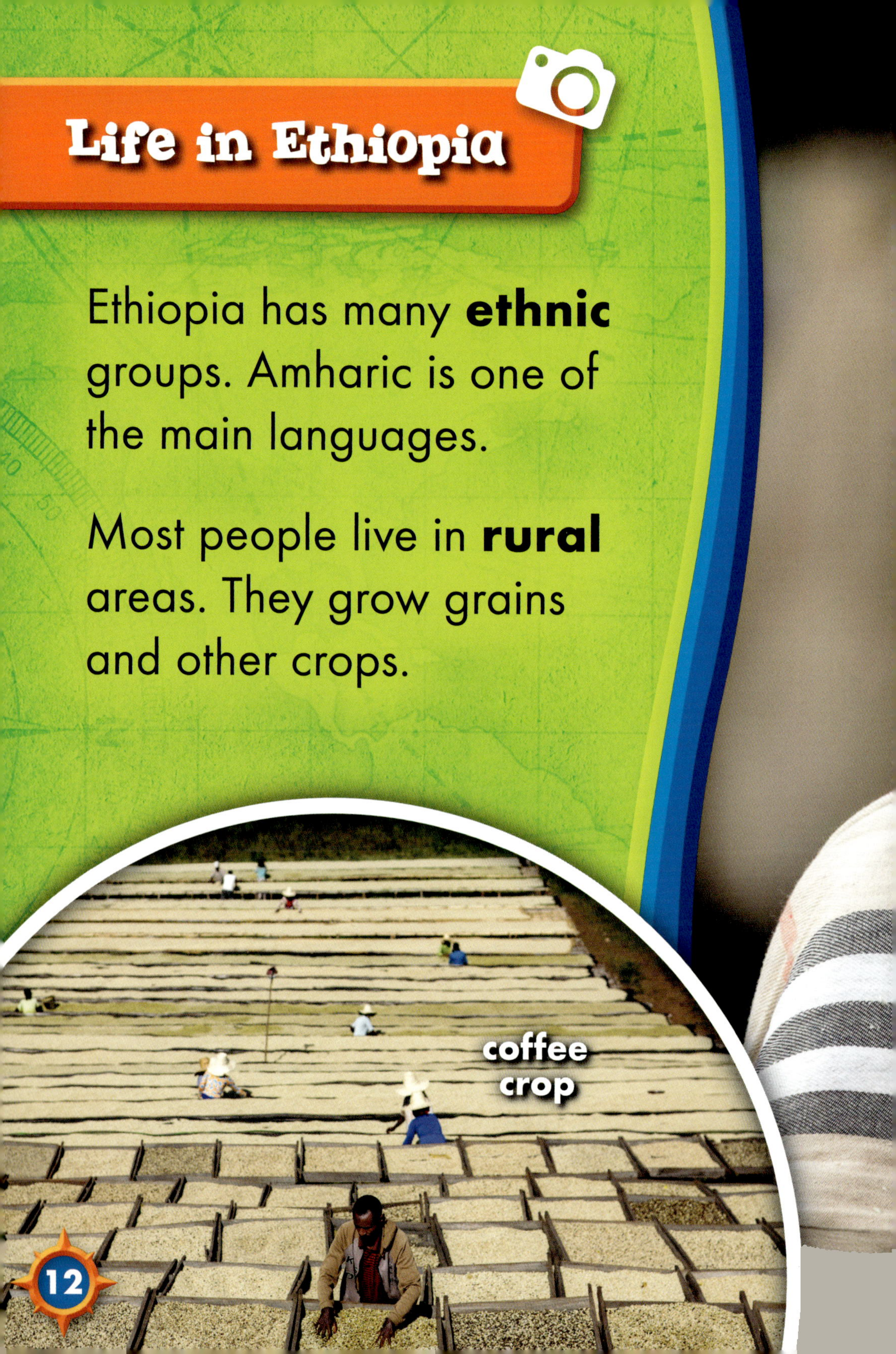

Life in Ethiopia

Ethiopia has many **ethnic** groups. Amharic is one of the main languages.

Most people live in **rural** areas. They grow grains and other crops.

coffee crop

English: Hello
Amharic: Selam
(sah-LAHM)

Music is popular in Ethiopia. The *eskista* is a **traditional** shoulder dance.

Track and field and soccer are favorite sports. Many people run in **marathons**.

Most meals are eaten with flatbread called *injera*. *Wot* is a stew with meat or vegetables.

Fuul is a dish made with mashed fava beans. *Tibs* is sliced beef.

Timkat is an important **festival**. Every January people pray and sing.

Enkutatash is the Ethiopian New Year. People give yellow flowers to one another. Ethiopians love their country!

Ethiopia Facts

Size:
426,373 square miles
(1,104,300 square kilometers)

Population:
118,550,298 (2024)

National Holiday:
Derg Downfall Day (May 28)

Main Languages:
Oromo, Amharic

Capital City:
Addis Ababa

Famous Face

Name: Tirunesh Dibaba

Famous For: setting world records and winning Olympic gold medals for long-distance running

Religions

other: 2%

Protestant: 23%

Muslim: 31%

Ethiopian Orthodox: 44%

Top Landmarks

Aksum

Danakil Depression

Lalībela

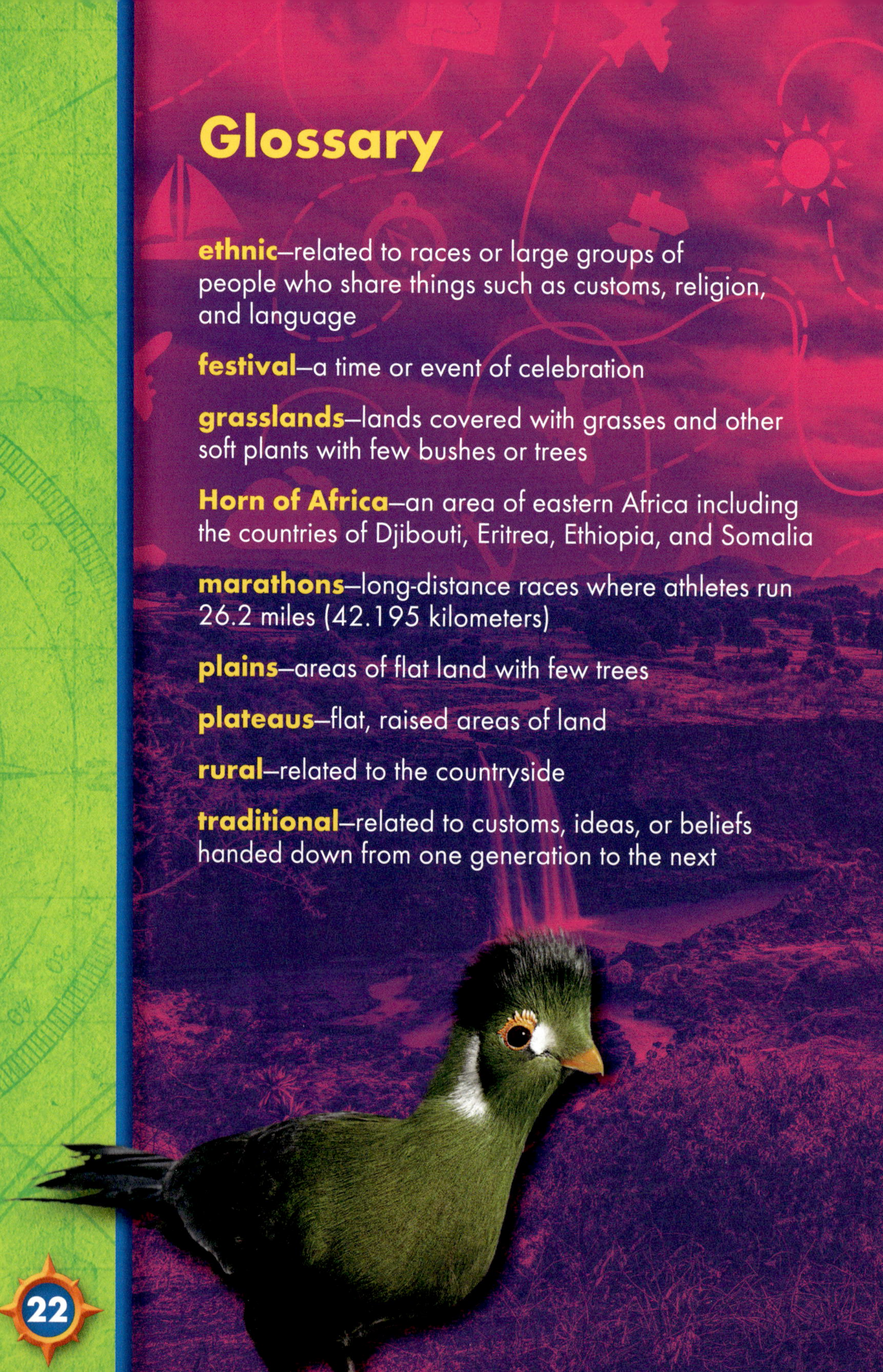

Glossary

ethnic—related to races or large groups of people who share things such as customs, religion, and language

festival—a time or event of celebration

grasslands—lands covered with grasses and other soft plants with few bushes or trees

Horn of Africa—an area of eastern Africa including the countries of Djibouti, Eritrea, Ethiopia, and Somalia

marathons—long-distance races where athletes run 26.2 miles (42.195 kilometers)

plains—areas of flat land with few trees

plateaus—flat, raised areas of land

rural—related to the countryside

traditional—related to customs, ideas, or beliefs handed down from one generation to the next

To Learn More

AT THE LIBRARY

Bolte, Mari. *Baboons.* Mankato, Minn.: Creative Education and Creative Paperbacks, 2025.

DiStasio, Nancy. *Ethiopia.* New York, N.Y.: Cavendish Square Publishing, 2022.

Orr, Tamra B. *Awesome Animals of Africa.* Mount Joy, Pa.: Curious Fox Books, 2024.

ON THE WEB

FACTSURFER

Factsurfer.com gives you a safe, fun way to find more information.

1. Go to www.factsurfer.com.
2. Enter "Ethiopia" into the search box and click 🔍.
3. Select your book cover to see a list of related content.

Index

The images in this book are reproduced through the courtesy of: WitR, front cover, pp. 6, 6-7; Mini Onion, p. 3; Matyas Rehak, p. 4; Framalicious, p. 8; Bluerain, p. 9; Tatyana Druzhinina, p. 10; Giedriius, pp. 11 (gelada, Ethiopian wolf); WitR, p. 11 (Walia ibex); Charlotte Bleijenberg, p. 11 (white-cheeked turaco); ERIC LAFFORGUE/ Alamy Stock Photo, p. 12; Hemis/ Alamy Stock Photo, pp. 12-13; Ivan Batinic/ Alamy Stock Photo, p. 14; aman ahmed ahmed, p. 15; Stewart Innes, p. 16 (injera); Linda Hughes Photography, p. 16 (wot); Alexander Mychko/ Alamy Stock Photo, p. 16 (fuul); Sergii Koval, p. 16 (tibs); Boaz Rottem/ Alamy Stock Photo, p. 17; LUIS TATO/ Contributor/ Getty Images, pp. 18-19; ZUMA Press, Inc./ Alamy Stock Photo, p. 20; travelview, p. 21 (Aksum); Katja Tsvetkova, p. 21 (Danakil Depression); John Grummitt, p. 21 (Lal bela); Eric Isselee, p. 22.